P... and the False Self

Finding Identity in God through Centering Prayer

Simon J Taylor
Director of Mission and Ministry Support,
Diocese of Bristol

GROVE BOOKS LIMITED
RIDLEY HALL RD CAMBRIDGE CB3 9HU

Contents

Acknowledgments

This book began life as sermons for Holy Week at All Saints Clifton in Bristol. I am grateful to Fr Charles Sutton, the churchwardens and the community at ASC for the invitation, welcome and engagement. Thank you to Jacky and Jes Taylor for proof reading (Ruth was dancing), and to Jane Gibbs and Ian Silk from the Grove team for patience and support.

First Impression November 2022
ISSN 0262-799X
ISBN 978 1 78827 277 3

1 Introduction

> 'What is truth? said jesting Pilate and would not stay for an answer'
> Francis Bacon[1]

Post-truth

In 2016, the *Oxford English Dictionary*'s word of the year was 'post-truth.' The definition it offered was this: 'circumstances in which objective facts are less influential in shaping public opinion than appeals to emotion and personal belief.' 2016 was the year of Brexit, when a bus carried the (erroneous) claim-*cum*-promise that 'We send the EU £350 million a week, let's fund our NHS instead.' During the referendum campaign, government minister Michael Gove claimed, 'People in this country have had enough of experts.'[2] 2016 was also the year of Donald Trump's election as President of the United States. After his inauguration in January 2017, one of Trump's aides coined the phrase 'alternative facts' to explain how Trump could be correct about something demonstrably untrue. Post-truth is a political reality, reflecting not so much that people are lying but rather that they care less about what is true than what is convenient and appealing to their supporters.

Beyond politics, post-truth is a cultural reality. A multi-million-dollar misinformation industry has grown up, which began with the tobacco industry. More recently similar tactics have been used by those who want to deny the reality of climate change. These tactics are to sow doubt in the scientific consensus, enlarging disagreement so that action which would be financially harmful to the industry is delayed or avoided. We see this used regularly by lobbyists, politicians and interest groups.

Post-truth is both a political and a cultural phenomenon. It is also an interpersonal one. Social media has exacerbated this. The algorithms which form the basis of most social media have two main effects: they connect us to people who are like us, and they show us material designed to provoke outrage and keep us on their webpage. Given that content on social media is short (280 characters or a short paragraph with a picture), the complexity of different opinions is lost. We share simplistic opinions with the like-minded, and fail to understand those who hold a different view. In our echo chambers, we provoke one another to ever greater self-righteous outrage towards those who disagree with us.

The dangers of a post-truth world are clear. Politically, we have seen the denial of election results, and an increase in political violence such that two Members of Parliament have been murdered since 2016. Globally, we see a strong-man leader who describes the invasion of a country led by a Jewish president as 'de-Nazification.' We live amidst a climate emergency, yet there is no concerted plan to address it. Social media trolling leads to suicides and death threats. The post-truth world is very dangerous.

Facing the Post-truth World

This post-truth world is not just the fault of other people, the political system or social media companies. We are all implicated. Evan Davis writes that while 'the era of post-truth politics is characterized by a willingness on the part of politicians to peddle reassuring myths, it is also marked by a readiness on the part of many voters to rise to these myths.'[3] The term post-truth was first used by the Serbian-American writer Steve Tesich in 1992. Reflecting on the United States following the political scandals of Watergate and the Iran-Contra affair, Tesich wrote that 'In a very fundamental way we, as a free people, have freely decided that we want to live in some post-truth world.'[4] We are complicit in post-truth. We prefer easy myths to hard truths, accept the reflection of our own desires in election promises, allow the ease of inaction to prevent change to our lifestyles, and seek out the reassurance of the like-minded rather than face into difficult debate. This is true of Christians as much as of others.

How do we change this situation? For a political, cultural and interpersonal reality, there are political, cultural and interpersonal aspects to our response. Each of those responses requires people who are deeply committed to living truthfully in a way that goes beyond the political and ethical response. In order to address the corrosive power of untruth on our selves and our society, we need a response that faces that corrosive power at its roots. We are ourselves complicit in post-truth. This goes deeper than our participation in the post-truth world and our rewarding of those who use post-truth to win our custom or our votes. It is rooted in an idolatrous and illusory understanding of who we are, which Thomas Merton called the 'false self.'[5] If we are to resist post-truth, then we need to up-root it from our deepest and truest self.

The False and True Self

Thomas Merton (1915–1968) was an American monk who sought to bring the riches of the Christian contemplative tradition to a wider audience. It is in his teaching about contemplation that Merton speaks of the false self.

> Every one of us is shadowed by an illusory person: a false self. This is the man [*sic*] that I want myself to be but who cannot exist, because

God does not know anything about him. And to be unknown of God is altogether too much privacy. My false and private self is the one who wants to exist outside the reach of God's will and God's love—outside reality and outside of life. And such a self cannot help but be an illusion.[6]

For Merton, the false self is the person I would like to be; it is a projection of my own fantasy and wishful thinking. Richard Rohr puts this well. 'Our false self is who we *think* we are. It is our mental self-image and social agreement, which most people spend their whole lives living up to—or down to. It is a fictional creation. It will die when we die. It is endlessly fragile, needy and insecure.'[7] The false self is a product of our own ego and fantasy. It is rooted in the falsehood that we are in control of our lives.

Most insidiously, the false self can lie behind even some of our best actions. Those whom Jesus describes as drawing attention to their almsgiving, or praying to be seen by others, are performing good actions out of their false selves (Matt 6.2–5). Christians are certainly not immune to it. Indeed, the desire to present ourselves as good and godly Christians is a way in which the false self operates in us.

But the false self is an illusion, and does not exist. Merton is emphatic that the false self cannot exist because in its very nature it is a fantasy. Because it is fantasy and untrue, God cannot know this self. Apart from God it cannot exist. Yet we cling to our illusions about ourselves; we cling to our false selves. Here, our collusion with our false self becomes idolatrous and sinful. As we seek to care for this false self, we find that the demands of ego, the need to meet expectations and to maintain appearances, make the false self into the totality of our world. Merton writes that 'All sin starts from the assumption that my false self, the self that exists only in my egocentric desires, is the fundamental reality of life to which everything else in the universe is ordered.'[8] Elsewhere, Merton writes 'The sinful self is not my real self, it is not the self you have wanted for me, only the self that I have wanted for myself.'[9]

What we need to combat the false self looks very like St Paul's account of judgment in which our work will be 'revealed with fire, and the fire will test what sort of work has been done' (1 Cor 3.13).[10] The false self cannot survive this test; it burns away quicker than straw. 'If the work is burned,' Paul continues, 'the builder will suffer loss; the builder will be saved, but only as through fire' (1 Cor 3.15). If our false self will be burned away, Merton suggests that this is because it had no reality in the first place. What remains is our true self, the self that is real because it is known by God. Merton speaks of 'allowing God to strip us of our false selves and make us into the new [people] that we are really meant to be.'[11] Our true identity 'is hidden in the love and mercy of God.'[12]

Centering Prayer

Thomas Merton wrote of the false self in the context of teaching about contemplative prayer. The false self is both revealed and stripped away in prayer. I will end each chapter of this book with a spiritual practice that will help us to strip away the false self and return to truthfulness. It is by engaging in these practices that we will, by God's grace, become people of integrity who can resist the lure and the lies of post-truth culture.

Foundational to this stripping away of the false self is the practice of centering prayer, developed by Thomas Keating as 'The contemplative dimension of the gospel.'[13] Centering prayer asks us simply to be in the presence of God. In silence we are present to God, putting aside everything that comes to us. It is a prayer of consent to what God will work in us, founded upon trust in the goodness of God. This prayer brings healing and blessing, but these are not experienced during the time of prayer, but rather in our ongoing lives. Keating describes centering prayer as 'a journey into the unknown. It is a call to follow Jesus out of all the structures, security blankets, and even spiritual practices that serve as props for the ego. They are all left behind insofar as they are part of or under the influence of the false-self system.'[14]

Spiritual Exercise—Centering Prayer

- Find a short word or phrase (*eg* Jesus, Father, Mother, Amen, Love, Be still). Keating calls this a 'sacred word.' We use the sacred word to re-centre ourselves when we are distracted.
- Sit or kneel comfortably, uncrossing all your limbs. Make sure your back is well supported. Be relaxed and alert.
- Set a timer for 20 minutes (or as long as you are happy to spend in silence).
- Ask God to strip away your false self.
- Close your eyes and let go of all conscious thought.
- Use the sacred word to re-centre yourself whenever you are distracted.
- At the end, thank God for this time and for God's work in your life.

2

Called to be Truthful

> A truth that's told with bad intent
> Beats all the lies you can invent
>
> William Blake[15]

Our true self is who God has made us to be, and who God also calls us to be. God calls us to truth, and to be freed from the grip of our false selves. Responding to God's call does not make us into cardboard cut-out Christians, all the same as one another. It is the false self, laden with ego and wanting to be who we think others want us to be, that produces sameness. God's call to us leads us into ever more uniqueness as we discover the beauty and complex truth of being who we are called to be—our true selves. This is not an easy thing to do.

Lies begin with small deviations from the truth. The serpent in the Garden of Eden begins with a small twist of the truth before the bigger lie (Gen 3.1–5). Stephen Long notices that 'The father of lies knows that the words he utters are not exactly what God said; they have been slightly altered…But in slightly twisting the divine word, the crafty serpent sows a seed of doubt in Eve's mind.'[16] The illusions of the false self are, in their origins, a subtle twisting of the goodness of our true selves.

Jesus Tempted

We see all of this at work in the beginning of Jesus' ministry. Having been baptized by John in the River Jordan, Jesus is impelled by the Holy Spirit into the wilderness (Mark 1.12; Matt 4.1; Luke 4.1–2). Notice that it is the Holy Spirit who does this. In the wilderness, Jesus fasts, prays and is tempted. Matthew and Luke record three temptations—to turn stones into bread, to take authority over the whole world, and to throw himself off the Temple. Notice again that these are all good things, and things that Jesus goes on to do.

The first temptation is to make bread out of stones. Jesus is hungry, and there were many hungry people in Palestine and Israel in his day, as in ours. Making bread and feeding the hungry would be good things. Later, Jesus makes bread for 5,000 and 4,000 people at a time. But in the wilderness, Jesus tells the tempter that we do not live by bread alone.

Then Jesus is tempted to take power over all the kingdoms of the world. Jesus in charge; surely that is a good thing. With Jesus in charge of the world, the fighting in Ukraine would end and there would be justice and peace throughout the world. At the end of St Matthew's gospel, Jesus tells his disciples that 'All authority in heaven and on earth has been given to me' (Matt 28.18), yet in the wilderness Jesus refuses the devil's offer and responds that we are to worship only God.

Finally, Jesus is taken to the pinnacle of the Temple and tempted to throw himself off to prove God's power. After all, does not the Bible say that God will command angels to protect you? Throughout his ministry, Jesus will prove God's power in his teaching, his healing, his raising of Lazarus from the dead, and by his own resurrection. Yet in the wilderness Jesus tells the devil not to put God to the test.

Tempted by Good Things

Three temptations, all to do good things, all things Jesus will later do, and all rejected. That should make us look deeper. Jesus is sent to the wilderness by the Holy Spirit, immediately following his baptism when God declares that 'You are my Son, the beloved, in whom I am well pleased' (Mark 1.11; Matt 3.17; Luke 3.22). The wilderness is where Jesus can explore what this means, and who God has called him to be. The temptations are all connected to this—they are all distorted versions of his true calling. St Ignatius Loyola reportedly said that 'The good are tempted by the good.' It is no good tempting me to do something I consider to be dreadful; I will resist. But great tragedies have resulted from people on a crusade for what is good. Even if there is no crusade, I can be warped and moulded little by little in directions that are profoundly wrong.

The wilderness is where Jesus can explore who God has called him to be

Returning to the wilderness, the temptation to turn stones into bread asks Jesus to gratify his own desires, and treat the world as something that exists only for him. This is a temptation to an entitled approach to the world, to become a person who takes what he wants, rather than a person who wants what God has to give. If he will change stones into bread, what will he do to people? Jesus resists this temptation, pointing to the deeper food that the word of God will give.

The temptation to take power would involve worshipping the devil, rather than going to the cross. Power is a major distortion in so many callings. We take power, often to do good things, but are distorted by what we do to get power. Jesus refuses to take power at the expense of worshipping that which is not God.

The third temptation, to prove God's care, is rooted in a place of insecurity, fear and doubt. Jesus has been told that he is God's beloved son; the devil tempts him to test that. Insecurity and fear make us do things that end up in taking what we want, and they make us take power at any cost to cover up our insecurity and fear.

Resources to Resist Temptation

To be called by God in a post-truth world means to resist the temptations to gratify our immediate desires, and to question entitlement when we see it. It means to resist temptations to give our allegiance in return for power, and to question whom those with power ultimately serve. It is to trust in the basic truth of being beloved by God, and helping others to know that belovedness in place of the insecurity and fear of our culture. The temptations of gratification, power and insecurity distort the goodness of our call. They draw us away from our true selves and into the illusions of the false self.

Truth is discovered in the patient and costly resistance to these temptations of our false selves. Only by dying to our false selves can we find the truth of our calling, and speak truth in our post-truth world. The gospel story gives us resources to deal with these temptations.

Only by dying to our false selves can we find the truth of our calling

To the temptation of self-gratification, the gospel shows us Jesus fasting. Jesus does not always fast; indeed he is later known as a 'winebibber and a glutton' (Matt 11.19, AV). Fasting helps us to be in tune with what we really and deeply hunger for, not simply what will satisfy our urges and immediate desires. Fasting takes us beyond self-gratification to what we truly long for. As he wrestles with God's call, Jesus fasts and withstands the temptation to turn stones into bread.

To the temptation of power, the gospel shows us Jesus in the wilderness, away from the centre of power, and away from other people. This is where the Holy Spirit has taken him. Here the temptation of power has less purchase, away from the gravitational forces of other people and powerful institutions. Here Jesus can refuse the devil's offer of all the kingdoms of the world, because he can see the cost of that offer.

To the temptation of insecurity and self-doubt, the gospel shows us Jesus declared to be the beloved Son of God. Whether a public statement or a private experience (the text can be read either way), it is a reality. Jesus' confidence in his identity as beloved enables him to refuse the devil's invitation to put God to the test.

As we seek to follow the call of God to be our true selves, we need these resources of fasting, wilderness and belovedness. Fasting can be missing a meal or not eating anything for twenty-four hours. For some, fasting from food will be unhealthy or unhelpful. Fasting could equally be fasting from shopping or using social media. Fasting helps us to identify what it is for which we are truly hungry. It helps us to withstand the temptations of self-gratification.

Wilderness takes us away from the normal places of our lives and to places on the margins of society. For some Christians, taking a retreat is a regular way of getting away from the normal. For others, time spent with those on the margins helps us to see the cost of what has become normal for us. We need to spend time in the wilderness, so that we may withstand the temptations of power.

Finally, we need to be secure in our identity as those loved by God. This belovedness is fed by centering prayer. Centering prayer is an encounter with the God who loves us and longs for us. In the silence of centering prayer, we are in the presence of God and in the presence of truth—the truth that God loves us.

Spiritual Exercises— Fasting, Retreat, Centering Prayer

- How might you fast in order to identify your true hunger, and to move away from self-gratification?
- Where might you go to find wilderness or retreat that is away from the normal and away from places and people of power?
- Try centering prayer once more (see chapter one). As you enter the silence, hear again the words of God: 'You are my beloved son, my beloved daughter, in whom I am well pleased.

3

True Prayer

> It's very important for Christians to be honest with God…
> God is much more interested in who you are than who you want to be.
>
> Bono[17]

Prayer is at the heart of what it means to be truthful people, what it means to follow Jesus, the way, the truth and the life. In our post-truth world, truth is regularly undermined. This is reinforced by media and social media, and undermines and corrupts all aspects of our lives. Behind this is what Thomas Merton called our false selves, our egocentric illusory selves who dominate what we do for so much of the time. To follow Jesus, to be truthful, means to be freed from the grip of our false selves. Only then will we be able to witness to truth in our post-truth world. But even in prayer, the false self is at work.

Two Pray-ers

Jesus told a story of two people at prayer (Luke 18.9–14). The first is a Pharisee, someone for whom attending the Temple, reading the Scriptures and doing the right things were very important. Pharisees were, we might say, the churchgoers of Jesus' day. What we learn from the Pharisee of the story is that the false self is at work even when we are praying. The self that the Pharisee brings to prayer is an illusion; it separates him from others ('I thank you that I am not like other people'), it relies on his own activity ('I fast…I give tithes'). Notice too that this is a long prayer, far longer than the tax collector's. The Pharisee is presenting to God a self that is a fantasy, a false self. Thomas Merton tells us that because the false self is an illusion and wants to exist 'outside the reach of God's will and God's love' therefore 'God does not know anything about [them].'[18] God does not hear the Pharisee's prayer, because God does not know the false self who prays.

Tax collectors in Jesus' time were collaborators with the occupying Romans. Taxes were farmed, and tax collectors would pay the Romans what they asked for and make a profit on top. That made tax collectors unpopular (to say the least) and meant they lived on the fringe of religious society, perpetually associating with unclean foreigners and becoming unclean themselves. No wonder the tax collector stood 'far off' (Luke 18.13). The tax collector's prayer is short, pleading and, above all, honest and true. 'God, be merciful to me, a sinner' (Luke 18.13). It is this prayer that Jesus says is heard by God.

Praying truthfully needs, above all, three things: silence, confession and lament. We need more than that: we need the word of God, praise and intercession as well. But silence, confession and lament are underplayed and underused in the church today, so I will concentrate on them.

Silence

Silence and the contemplative tradition of Christianity is one of the great gifts we have to offer a world mired in post-truth. In silent prayer, we rest in the presence of the God who loves us and we simply are. There is no need to do anything to get God's attention or love. There is no need to be anything other than who we are, which is to say loved by God. In silent prayer we allow the presence of God to fill us and infuse us. This heals us, allowing God into the deepest and most broken parts of us to make them whole. Rowan Williams describes this prayer as like sunbathing.[19] Sunbathing in prayer has the effect of burning off our false selves, as the sun burns away the morning mist. Silent prayer brings us into contact with our truest selves, and can therefore be discomforting. Sarah Coakley describes silent prayer as 'the destruction of false idolatry,' and this can be a difficult experience.[20] But it is rooted in the presence of the God who loves us, and returns us to that presence. Silent prayer transforms us, and enables us to become our true selves.

Confession

Confession is at the heart of the tax collector's prayer. It is, and should be, a regular part of our prayers when we gather together. Truthful prayer requires confession, requires us to acknowledge that we have sinned and that we need God's help to turn away from sin. Even here the false self can be at work, being secretly proud that we are not the kind of person that sins in particular ways, or proud that we are able to make such a full confession. When we come to confession, we come as sinners who need forgiveness. We stand on nothing more than that need for forgiveness. We need to let go of our justifications (the spiritual equivalent of 'I'm sorry you felt offended by that') and acknowledge truly that we have done wrong, that it has hurt others and ourselves, that we want to change, and that we need God's help to do so. Making an individual confession to another Christian or (in some church traditions) to a priest can be a powerful way of being truthful in prayer, but should not be—and is not—a requirement (there is an old adage about personal confession that 'all can, none must, and some should').

Lament

Lament is not a very British way of conducting ourselves, but it is very biblical. In the Bible we see Abraham, Moses, the prophets and Jesus lamenting. An entire book of the Bible is named for Lamentations. Above all it is in the psalms that we find lament. 'How long, O Lord? Will you forget me for ever?' begins Psalm 13. 'O God, why do you cast us off for ever? Why does your anger smoke against the sheep of your pasture?' says Psalm 74, and of course famously Psalm 22 begins, 'My God, my God, why have you forsaken me?' There is nothing held back in the prayers of the psalms.

Lament is a form of honesty. In lament we come before God as we are and say what we really think. This can be anger, pain, sadness or sorrow. Lament is a mixture of all of these. Lament is truthful presence to God following something that has hurt, disturbed or wounded us. Lament is the prayer we need following a bereavement or a disaster. David Runcorn tells a story of lament disrupting our overly neat way of being Christian.

> ...from the back came a loud voice with a strong Australian accent: 'Lord, I just don't know what you're playing at. What are you doing?' The honest directness of the prayer cut across the whole service. I was caught between a guilty resentment that our warm joy had been broken into, and relief that a terrible burden of truth had been offered to God. We had not known how—or even whether—we could. The speaker had only recently become a Christian. He had not yet learned how Christians usually pray about such things. I hope he never does.[21]

Silence, confession and lament are three ingredients of truthful praying, three things that will enable us to witness to truth in a post-truth world. These are not techniques; the false self can be at work in all of them. Rather, if we approach them with honesty, they are means by which, through God's grace, we cultivate a deeper relationship with God.

To return to Jesus' story of the Pharisee and the tax collector, notice how it relates to the Lord's Prayer, itself a deeply truthful prayer. Whereas the Pharisee distances himself from other people, the Lord's Prayer begins, '*Our* Father.' Where the Pharisee speaks of his own deeds and being, the Lord's Prayer points to God: 'Hallowed be *Thy* name, *Thy* kingdom come, *Thy* will be done.' With the tax collector, the Lord's Prayer comes from a place of dependence on God, 'Give us this day our daily bread,' and asks for God's mercy: 'Forgive us our trespasses as we forgive those who trespass against us.' And above all, the Lord's Prayer is honest about things being hard: 'Lead us not into temptation, but deliver us from evil.'

Spiritual Exercises—Silence, Confession, Lament

- Return again to centering prayer (see chapter one). Can you treat the silence as sunbathing?
- What is your regular practice of confession? What might you do to deepen it?
- Read a psalm of lament (try Psalm 13, 22 or 74). Then try writing a psalm of lament yourself. Do not hold back; God can take it.

4

Truth at Night

> Out of them came another horn, a little one, which grew exceedingly great... it cast truth to the ground, and kept prospering in what it did.
>
> Dan 8.9, 12

According to the Christian socialist preacher Ethel Annakin, the first casualty of war is truth. As we seek to be people of truth in a culture of post-truth, we have to be able to see and hold to truth even when life is hard. In the darkness of suffering, evil, confusion and fear, truth remains important. There is huge suffering in our world. As I write, the war in Ukraine involves killing, rape and other horrors. There are other, unreported and forgotten wars in Yemen, South Sudan, Ethiopia, Nigeria, Mali and many more places. There is starvation in Afghanistan, and food poverty in the UK. There is suffering and death faced by those we know and love dearly. Within our own selves we can see darkness—selfishness, vindictiveness, jealousy.

Truth in the Dark

In the midst of darkness, it can be hard to see the truth. The dark conceals things, through the complexity of understanding what is really going on, and through the deep fog of pain and suffering. Darkness conceals truth; evil distorts truth. A fragment or incomplete truth can be twisted into a falsehood. We have already seen that the serpent in Genesis 3 does this. As one commentator puts it, 'The subtle serpent creates a disorienting atmosphere of uncertain questions.'[22] A further concealment comes in the injustice seen when those who speak falsehood and do awful things benefit from them. It can even seem that God is powerless. Jeremiah makes this a complaint against God: 'Why does the way of the guilty prosper? Why do all who are treacherous thrive?' (Jer 12.1). In the dark, it may even appear God is absent and has abandoned us.

The false self thrives when we stray from the truth in the dark. We are tempted to become heroic figures fighting the darkness and conquering injustice. We may be tempted to give up, to complain that the world is against us and no one can help us. Our false selves become emboldened when we are faced with hardship and suffering. We seek the false comfort of heroism or victimhood, and lose sight of the truth that even here we are beloved of God.

Revealing God's Glory

At the pivotal moment in his gospel, John simply says, 'It was night' (John 13.30). Judas has left to betray Jesus, and now it is night. Now it is the time for deeds of evil, for suffering and death. Jesus will be betrayed, abandoned, denied, accused, tortured, condemned, crucified and will die. In the night, with the door barely closed on Judas leaving to betray him, Jesus announces, 'Now the Son of Man has been glorified, and God has been glorified in him' (John 30.31). It is at the moment that evil, suffering and death seem be at their strongest that Jesus announces his glory.

The glory of God is a theme throughout the Bible. The people of Israel see the glory of God on the top of Mount Sinai, and in the pillar of cloud that leads them through the wilderness. In Jesus we see the glory of God; Jesus is the visible presence of the invisible God (Col 1.15). We see the glory of God most clearly in the night in which Jesus is betrayed, condemned and executed. So strongly is this theme in the gospels, that Matthew, Mark and Luke all speak of the curtain of the Temple—which hung in front of the Holy of Holies where the glory of God lived—torn from top to bottom when Jesus died. The presence of God was now most fully seen in the dead Jesus. Archbishop Michael Ramsey grasped this when he said that 'Calvary is no disaster which needs the resurrection to reverse it, but a victory to signal that the resurrection follows quickly to seal it.'[23]

Where the darkness conceals truth, the glory of God reveals it

Where the darkness conceals truth, the glory of God reveals it. When we speak of glory, our false selves think of fame, acclaim and drama. True glory, the glory that was revealed in the night after Judas had left the table, is the presence of God. God is present in the suffering and death of Jesus, and God is present in the suffering and death of all God's children. The invisible God is present in holding the hand of someone who is in pain or scared, or as the care worker enables someone to wash in dignity. We need to train ourselves to see this true glory, small, hidden and futile as it might seem, and not the superficial, heroic and dramatic glory that appeals to our false selves.

Later in the night that Judas initiates, Jesus asks his disciples to 'Watch with me one hour. Watch and pray that you may not enter into temptation' (Mark 14.37–38). There is not much drama in watching and praying. It is not something from which our false selves can make gains. So the disciples fall asleep. In a similar way, Paul's instructions on spiritual warfare are simply to 'stand.' In fact, he repeats this instruction four times (Eph 6.11–14). Paul does not tell Christians to rush into battle, wielding the sword of the Spirit and taking on the enemy. He simply asks us to stand and to withstand. This is not a battle we have to win, but one that we have to endure. Watching and standing are not the heroic acts that our false selves find glamorous (although even here the false self can find ways to boast in the length of time we have watched or the trials we have endured while we stood). Above all, they do not lead to winning, and there is little the false self loves more than a victory. The only winning we are to do is to win our neighbour. St Anthony, the earliest monastic teacher, says that 'Our life and our death is with our neighbour. If we win our brother we win God. If we cause our brother to stumble we have sinned against Christ.'[24]

A Two-fold Movement

As we confront our false self in the dark, we need to own and let go of all that is untrue and distorts us. This is not a heroic purging of our darkness, a kind of spiritual boot camp, but an ongoing owning and accepting of what there is within us that distorts us, and a patient letting go of it. This owning and letting go allows us to receive what is good and true, and to reject distortion into untruth. It undoes the serpent's work. This is a twofold action, first owning and then letting go. Confession has this shape, owning what we have done and letting it go into God's forgiveness.

Another discipline with this shape is welcoming prayer. Welcoming prayer embraces painful emotions and experiences. It welcomes them in, and by doing so sees them for what they are. Having welcomed them in, the next movement of the prayer releases them and lets them go. In a moment of anger, I might say, 'Anger, I recognize and welcome you.' Saying that gives me a moment of pause, after which I can make the conscious choice to say 'Anger, I release you and let you go.' This values the anger as a healthy and proper response to what provokes it, but releases it before it controls me and turns into resentment or violence. It is a powerful prayer. Thomas Keating describes it as 'The practice that actively lets go of thoughts and feelings that support the false-self system.'[25]

Truthfulness at night is most important in our post-truth world. It is when things are hard, when we are in the presence of suffering, evil and death, that we most need to be truthful, and where our false selves will make a strong bid to take charge. Being truthful at night means learning to see the glory of God; it means standing and watching with Jesus; and it means owning and letting go of all that distorts and harms us.

Spiritual Exercise—the Welcoming Prayer

- Practise the welcoming prayer with a small frustration or annoyance.
- Begin by welcoming the thoughts and feelings you are having.
- Name them one by one and welcome them.
- Then, naming the thoughts and feelings one by one, let them go.

5 The Body of Truth

> I'm gonna look twice at you
> until I see the Christ in you.
> When I'm lookin' through the eyes of love.
>
> The Waterboys[26]

Resisting Together

We are not asked to resist this post-truth culture on our own. It is something that we do together. Talking about the false self can easily become an individualistic exercise. The service of truth needs other people, to check what we are saying and thinking, to encourage us in our service, and to bring different perspectives that challenge and enlarge our understanding of truth. Matthew D'Ancona says that 'If post-truth is to be defied and defeated, the endeavour must be collective, sustained and stubborn.'[27] Remembering that we are people who depend on others, and on whom others depend, is a truth that cuts against the individualism and power grabbing of post-truth culture and the false self.

The Body of Christ

The church in Corinth was a mess. There were different factions, arguments over how worship should happen, arguments over how marriage should be considered in the church and more. At the heart of the letter was not an argument but a practice—the practice of sharing bread and wine. This practice should have been about remembering the night when Jesus was betrayed and proclaiming the death of Jesus. But what was actually happening was that as they came together to worship and to share bread and wine, some were having a full meal with plenty to drink while others had nothing. 'One goes hungry and another becomes drunk' (1 Cor 11.21).

To counter this, Paul begins by reminding the Corinthians of the story of the Last Supper and goes on to speak about the need to 'discern the body,' to recognize the body of Christ when we gather to share bread and wine (1 Cor 11.23–26). This comes as a warning—'Anyone who eats and drinks without discerning the body eats and drinks judgment upon themselves' (1 Cor 11.29). This introduces Paul's great theme about being the body of Christ. We are all one body, Paul teaches, made one by the Spirit in one baptism, whatever our background (1 Cor 12.12–13). But that does not make us the same. Paul at his funniest continues, 'If the foot were to say, 'Because I am not a hand, I do not belong to the body,' that would not make it any less a part of the body. And if the ear were to say, 'Because I am not an eye, I do not belong to the body,' that would not make it any less a part of the body' (1 Cor 12.15–16). The comedy makes Paul's point—we are obviously different, and we all belong together. After this lengthy chapter teaching about the body, Paul concludes by writing the famous hymn to love that is one of the best-known passages of the whole Bible (1 Cor 13). We need love if we are to be the body of Christ.

I notice two things here. First, we can think that arguments and problems in the church are a recent thing. They are not—they go back to the very earliest church. And secondly, I thank God for these arguments and problems. They have led to the Letter to the Corinthians and Paul's fantastic teaching. Our false selves like to think we are special and unique, but arguments have been in the church for as long as there has been a church. Our false selves like things to be sorted out, preferably by doing it ourselves, but thanking God for problems is not consistent with this.

The Gifts and Dangers of the Church

We need to face the fact that the church is a place where our false selves can have a field day. The church can be, and has been, a very dangerous place for some people. The church can be, and has been, a place where truthful following of Jesus is fatally undermined by our false selves. I want to look at the church through three lenses: the church as an institution, the church as a gathering, and the church as a body. For each, there are great gifts to celebrate, there are dangers that attract our false selves, and there are practices that can help us to unpack the gifts and avoid the dangers.

Church as Institution

First, the church as an institution, both as a local church or a larger institution—a circuit, diocese, district or a denomination. The gift here is of a spaciousness and breadth that allows for so many to be part of it. The danger is of elevating the institution above the people who are part of it. For our false selves, the glamour of the institution can make it seem more important than people. This has led to people being harmed in order to protect the church and its reputation.[28] The horrific stories that continue to be disclosed about safeguarding failures are just one dreadfully real aspect of this. For some, the glamour of the institution can lead our false selves to lose our identity within the institution. Again, this can be a danger locally (I am a member of St Martin's church) or at a wider level (I am an Anglican).

To unpack the gifts of the church as an institution, we need to practise honest truth-telling about failures whenever they happen. The church (like all institutions) is here for a purpose, a purpose that serves a greater good than itself. It is not here simply to be. It needs to be held to that purpose, to that greater good, as do its members and its leaders. We also need to remember our identities as people, distinct from roles and responsibilities. We need also to remember that those in leadership are also human beings, and pray for them by name rather than by their role.

Church as Gathering

The gifts of the church as a gathering are that it brings togetherness and fellowship. The dangers are that it excludes people and that gathered together we become inward looking and self-serving. One of the greatest failures of the Church of England, in which I serve, in recent times was during the Windrush immigration. People who had been loyal Anglicans all of their lives came to England and were told they were not welcome. Our gatherings were excluding, and serving our own social interests. Our false selves can have a riotous time, emulating the Pharisee who stood in the Temple and said, 'I'm glad I don't go to the same church as these people. I'm respectable.' I wonder who we might be excluding today, what of our own interests we might be serving?

If there is a practice that can help us to unpack the gifts of fellowship and togetherness that the church as a gathering can offer, then it may be to watch people come into church, or go up for communion, and give thanks for them—all of them. As we pray for those who are here, we might pray to see who is missing.

Church as Body

Finally, the church as a body. The gift here is of difference—all the myriad elements working together for the good of the body. We need to remember that this image comes out of argument and division. The danger here is not argument, it is that we will close down the argument and stop recognizing the other person as part of the body. Our false selves make this as easy as they can. I have come to recognize that there is a typically Church of England heresy, and like many heresies it is beguiling and subtle. It is also one that allows our false selves to feel good. Often told as a joke, it often obscures a deeper intention. The typical Church of England heresy is this—'You worship God in your way, and I'll worship God in his.' It is subtle, and it sounds inclusive. Our false selves love it. But it is not inclusive at all.

Two things can help us unpack the gifts that the church as a body has for us—the gifts of difference and working together. One is to be curious about what other people do and think. The other is to hold on as we argue—hold on to Jesus and what you see him doing in your thinking and acting, and hold on to the other person and Jesus at work in what they say and do. Others have important things to teach us about Jesus. We will need to practice curiosity and holding on together. We need to be curious about what makes another person think or do things you find difficult and to hold on to Jesus in yourself and in the other as you argue. If we can see that the other person is connected to Jesus, and therefore to us, we start to break down the polarization that is a feature of our post-truth world. It means that we allow Jesus working through the other person to break through our false selves.

Spiritual Exercise—Belonging to the Body

- Find someone in the church to which you belong who thinks about things differently from you.
- Ask them for a conversation, and listen with curiosity to what they say and why they say it.
- Pray with them and for them.

6 Resurrection Truth

> The truth is always more powerful than a lie.
>
> The Doctor[29]

Secular accounts of post-truth culture find their hope in the saying that 'truth will out.'[30] For secular commentators, this conviction that truth is enduring and ultimately will be recognized remains an assertion of hope. In the meantime, before the truth is finally recognized, there is a heavy price to pay for those who are attacked, made homeless or impoverished because of the denial of truth. Christian faith can give more substance to this conviction, and simultaneously can recognize the cost of the lie. The corrosive and damaging rejection of truth and the distorting and dehumanizing false self are revealed and overcome in the resurrection of Jesus.

The Lamb That was Slain

At the heart of a truly Christian response to post-truth culture is the resurrection of Jesus. In the Book of Revelation, when John has gone through the open door into heaven, one of the things he sees is 'A Lamb standing as though it had been slain' and thousands of angels singing 'Worthy is the Lamb who was slain to receive power and wealth and wisdom and might and honour and glory and blessing' (Rev 5.6, 12). It is certainly a strange sight—a slaughtered lamb standing up. It should remind us of the story of Jesus showing his wounds to Thomas—the risen Jesus still has the scars of his death (John 20.24–29). The resurrection is not the reversal of the crucifixion, an undoing of a tragic mistake. Rather, the resurrection shows us the truth that the crucifixion was God's victory over the powers of sin and death. This is the source of Christian hope and Christian joy.

The resurrection also gives us a basis for hope in the reality of truth being inscribed in creation. From the very beginning of creation we see the Bible telling of a God who made a world for peace and flourishing, not a world in which power and violence determine what is right and best. In the resurrection we are shown that God is seen most truly in the Lamb who was slain. God is not the strongest bully. God is the one who stands with the bullied, and whose love cannot be defeated by those with power and military hardware.[31]

Conversion

The resurrection shows us the truth about belonging. It brings us together as those who witness to Jesus. Jesus sends Mary Magdalene, whose love was constant even after his death, to find the others and to tell them that Jesus is alive (John 20.17). The stories of the risen Jesus forgiving and restoring his scattered friends and disciples are more about his spending time with them than about his imparting any more teaching. The resurrection brings us together to be the community of the resurrection—a body which reaches out to bring others into the joy of belonging with Jesus. This is a place where everyone can belong, where everyone can contribute, where everyone is loved and valued.

In this community, the resurrection shows us the truth about change, a change so profound that it can only be called conversion. Paul, who murdered the followers of Jesus, meets the risen Jesus and becomes an apostle. The ramshackle group of disciples go on to change the world, so that in less than three hundred years the whole Roman empire had become Christian. Resurrection brings conversion. Our hope is that even today's tyrants, liars and bullies can change.

With this, the resurrection shows us the truth about forgiveness. It is not just others who need to change. Here, through our baptism into the resurrection of Jesus, 'The false self is ritually put to death…in the death-dealing and life-giving waters of baptism.'[32] The image of the slaughtered Lamb standing in heaven is important because it invites us to return to the cross and see our part in the tyranny, the lies and the bullying. We need to be converted again and again. We can change. In the risen Jesus, the Lamb who was slain, we see our wrongdoing and we see that it does not have the last word. We are forgiven and invited to share in the praise of the Lamb. This is the source of our joy.

Death and Love

We are joyful because the resurrection shows us the truth about death. Jesus is alive. Death did not have the last word. Christians have trusted in the Lamb who was slain, and dared to speak the truth in the face of persecution and tyranny. Christian tradition says that all the first disciples were martyred for speaking about Jesus. The west front of Westminster Abbey has a series of ten statues of twentieth-century martyrs—amongst them are Esther John, killed for teaching about Jesus in Pakistan; Janani Luwum, murdered for resisting the tyranny of Idi Amin in Uganda; and Oscar Romero, murdered for speaking up for justice in El Salvador. All of them knew the Lamb who was slain, and so knew that death is not the last word.

In all of this we see that the resurrection shows us the truth about love. The resurrection is an act of love—the love of God for Jesus. The resurrection reveals an act of love—the love of Jesus for the world in dying for us all. The resurrection engenders acts of love without end—the love that we offer in response to the love of God and Jesus for us, for all people, for the whole of creation. There is no person who is not loved by God—wherever or whoever they are. There is no inch of creation that God does not love. There is no part of us that is not loved by God—whoever we are, whatever we are, we are loved by God. We have no need of our false self, the self that God does not know. God gives us our true self. As Thomas Merton says, 'In order to become myself I must cease to be what I always thought I wanted to be, and in order to find myself I must go out of myself, and in order to live I have to die.'[33] This is resurrection truth. We see all of this in the Lamb who was slain, the risen Jesus who is present with us here and now.

Spiritual Exercise—Joy

- Find something that makes you joyful. Give thanks to God for it.
- Sing a song of praise.

Short Bibliography

On Post-truth

M D'Ancona, *Post-truth: The New War on Truth and How to Fight Back* (London: Ebury, 2017).

E Davis, *Post-Truth: Peak Bullshit and What We Can Do About It* (London: Abacus, 2017).

D Stephen Long, *Truth Telling in a Post-truth World* (Nashville, TN: Foundery Books, 2019).

P Crumpler, *Responding to Post-truth* (Grove Ethics booklet E197).

On the False Self

T Merton, *Seeds of Contemplation* (Wheathampstead: Anthony Clarke, 1972).

R Rohr, *True Self, False Self*. Audiobook. (St Anthony Messenger Press, 2010).

On Centering Prayer

I Cowley, *The Contemplative Minister: Learning to Lead from the Still Centre* (Oxford: Bible Reading Fellowship, 2015).

T Keating, *Open Mind, Open Heart: The Contemplative Dimension of the Gospel* (London: Bloomsbury, 2006, 20th anniversary edition).

https://www.contemplativeoutreach.org/

Notes

1 F Bacon, *Essays* (London: Everyman Library, 1902) p 3.

2 Sky News, 3 June 2016.

3 E Davis, *Post-truth: Peak Bullshit and What We can Do About It* (London: Abacus, 2017) p 119.

4 S Teich, 'A Government of Lies,' *The Nation* January 6/13, 1992, p 13. Cited in M D'Ancona, *Post-truth: The New War on Truth and How to Fight Back* (London: Ebury, 2017) p 9.

5 Denys Turner traces the false self as least as far as Meister Eckhart (c1260–c 1328): 'For Eckhart, "my" self is not in the last resort *mine* at all. And any self which I can call my own is a false self, a self of possessive imagination' (D Turner, *The Darkness of God: Negativity in Christian Mysticism* (Cambridge University Press, 1995) p 184). My account of the false self is based on the work of Thomas Merton and his subsequent interpreters.

6 T Merton, *Seeds of Contemplation* (Wheathampstead: Anthony Clarke, 1972) p 27.

7 R Rohr, *Adam's Return: The Five Promises of Male Initiation* (New York: Crossroad 2004) p 43.

8 Merton, *Seeds of Contemplation, op cit*, p 27.

9 T Merton, *Thoughts in Solitude* (New York: Farrar, Straus and Cudahy, 1958) p 40.

10 All biblical quotations are from the New Revised Standard Version.

11 Merton, *Seeds of Contemplation, op cit*, p 183.

12 Merton, *Seeds of Contemplation, op cit,* p 28.

13 T Keating, *Open Mind, Open Heart: The Contemplative Dimension of the Gospel* (London: Bloomsbury, 2006, 20th anniversary edition).

14 *ibid,* pp 66–67.

15 W Blake, *Auguries of Innocence* (1803), in P Butler (ed), *William Blake* Everyman's Poetry (London: J M Dent, 1996) p 78.

16 D S Long, *Truth Telling in a Post-truth World* (Nashville, TN: Foundry Books, 2019) p 3.

17 M Saunders, 'Seven surprising things Bono has said about Jesus,' *Christian Today*, 13 November 2014, available at: https://www.christiantoday.com/article/seven-surprising-things-bono-has-said-about-jesus/42993.htm (accessed 3–4 January 2023).

18 Merton, *Seeds of Contemplation, op cit*, p 27.

19 *Pause for Thought*, Radio 2, Tuesday 18 October 2005.

20 S Coakley, *Powers and Submissions: Spirituality, Philosophy and Gender* (Oxford: Blackwell, 2002) p 38.

21 D Runcorn, *Choice, Desire and the Will of God: What More Do You Want?* (London: SPCK, 2003) p 110.

22 R R Reno, *Genesis* (London: SCM Press, 2010) p 85.

23 A M Ramsey, *The Glory of God and the Transfiguration of Christ* (London: Longmans, 1949) p 81.

24 Quoted in R Williams, *Silence and Honey Cakes: The Wisdom of the Desert* (Oxford: Lion, 2003) p 23.

25 Contemplative Outreach, 'Welcoming Prayer,' available at: https://www.contemplativeoutreach.org/welcoming-prayer-method/ (accessed 26 February 2023).

26 The Waterboys, 'Christ in You' (*Universal Hall*, 2003).

27 D'Ancona, *Post-truth, op cit*, p 146.

28 A helpful piece here is L Woodhead, 'Truth and Deceit in Institutions,' *Studies in Christian Ethics* 31(2022), pp 87–103.

29 *Doctor Who: Redacted* (BBC Sounds, 2022).

30 See, for example, Davies, *Post-truth, op cit*, p 299; D'Ancona, *Post-truth, op cit*, p 149.

31 I have written elsewhere about the biblical account of creation being opposed to the view that power and violence are determinative. See S J Taylor, *How to Read the Bible (without switching off your brain)* (London: SPCK, 2015) chapter 6.

32 Keating, *Open Mind, Open Heart, op cit*, p 159.

33 Merton, *Seeds of Contemplation, op cit*, p 37.